Lean Marketing

By Ade Asefeso MCIPS MBA

Second Edition

ISBN-13: 978-1499753790

ISBN-10: 1499753799

Publisher: AA Global Sourcing Ltd
Website: http://www.aaglobalsourcing.com

Table of Contents

4

Disclaimer

This publication is designed to provide competent and reliable information regarding the subject matter covered. However, it is sold with the understanding that the author and publisher are not engaged in rendering professional advice. The authors and publishers specifically disclaim any liability that is incurred from the use or application of contents of this book.

If you purchased this book without a cover you should be aware that this book may have been stolen property and reported as "unsold and destroyed" to the publisher. In this case neither the author nor the publisher has received any payment for this "stripped book."

Dedication

To my family and friends who seems to have been sent here to teach me something about who I am supposed to be. They have nurtured me, challenged me, and even opposed me.... But at every juncture has taught me!

This book is dedicated to my lovely boys, Thomas, Michael and Karl. Teaching them to manage their finance will give them the lives they deserve. They have taught me more about life, presence, and energy management than anything I have done in my life.

Chapter 1: Introduction

Lean Marketing is about being agile, about viewing each campaign or marketing activity as one step in the ever-improving progress towards customer acquisition and ultimately customer satisfaction.

Lean Marketing is a method to make you more effective than your competitors. Lean is something that some people want to do, to beat their competitors.

It is not something you have to do.

Lean Marketing is essentially a knowledge transfer system; it's a training system on how to define knowledge gaps and close them.

Lean Marketing takes an entirely different perspective on knowledge transfer. It is not the perspective of educating the customer; it is from the perspective of learning from the customer, understanding how your customer uses and benefits from your product or service.

Lean Marketing takes responsibility for demand. They are always in search for the next hassle map of the customer where tomorrow's demand exists.

Lean Marketing is targeted to certain kinds of organizations who actually enjoy learning. Who are committed to continuous improvement as opposed to just doing things and running things as they are.

Lean Marketing can be thought of as a strategic methodology to streamline and automate the marketing processes in order to improve efficiencies through waste elimination. Many Lean companies strive to eliminate, not minimize all waste in the process. Most think of this as only a manufacturing or administrative function. This rule can apply when implementing Lean marketing as well. In Lean marketing a company should only have two components; an introduction to a new lead and the acceptance of an order. All other components would be considered wasteful and are candidates for elimination. That may be a little to pie in the sky but I do not believe that marketing should not be off the hook from eliminating waste.

Here is a simple process to get started

The Six Step Process to Lean Marketing: How do you handle the critical elements of your Marketing or Value Stream and reduce waste in a lean flow?

1. Create a Value Stream Map based on your Marketing Flow.
2. Analyze each process and start asking these questions until you have eliminated all waste from the process:
   a. Why are we doing this process?
   b. What value/purpose does it serve the customer?
   c. How can we eliminate all waste from this process?
3. Map new simplified process:
   a. Now determine the constraint in your Marketing Flow.

b. Identify the system's constraint.

c. Exploit the system's constraint.

d. Subordinate everything else to the above decision.

e. Elevate the system's constraint.

f. If a constraint is broken (that is, relieved or improved), go back to Step 1. However, don't allow inertia to become a constraint.

4. Implement and Test new process using the Plan, Do, Check, Act cycle.

5. Simplify your Marketing Flow:

a. Eliminate all wasted activities that the customer sees little value in.

b. Create dashboard with input/output measurements showing daily, weekly, monthly and yearly progress.

c. Find the Value Stream ROI and Resource Allocation.

6. Create the Future Value Stream Map:

a. Feedback and develop visual metrics showing progress of the company's lean continuous improvement program.

Chapter 2: Setting Lean Marketing Goals

Why should you set clear goals?

It's not unusual for small business owners and entrepreneurs to focus on strategies and tactics at the expense of also setting appropriate goals. Often, this happens when you see someone else successfully executing a strategy or tactic and you try to duplicate their success by doing the same thing.

A small business that doesn't set clear long-term goals is doomed to fail.

Most small businesses – even successful small businesses fail to grow because the owners don't take the time to set meaningful goals. I've talked to thousands of small business owners. Most want to work for themselves and operate a business that will provide them and their families a good standard of living. But those aren't the goals I'm talking about. Most small business owners fail to set quarterly or yearly goals for their businesses. They simply operate the business, focusing on day to day activities, without establishing what they hope to accomplish within a certain amount of time. While your overall goal can be to make a ton of money and find enough free time to enjoy other activities, you should establish operating goals for your business.

Broad, long-term goals are important, but they rarely help you to evaluate the success or failure of focused strategies and tactics. For example, when we evaluated several years ago whether to participate on Twitter, Facebook and other social networks, we established five goals:

1. Find new customer prospects.
2. Build a community on each social network.
3. Build brand awareness about AA Global Sourcing.
4. Manage the perception of our brand.
5. Provide customer service.

We evaluated the success of our strategies and tactics in light of those five goals (we should have been more precise in our goal for how many new customer prospects we wanted to find). As you will notice, not all of our goals were quantitative. Most were qualitative and that is okay.

Goals can be quantitative (drive x visitors to the site over y period of time) or they can be qualitative (build a community of entrepreneur-customers), but they must be clearly defined and they must, at least in part, be measurable. How can a marketer measure progress against a stated goal unless they have some yardstick to use for comparison, whether that is indeed the number of visitors or the level of customer engagement as determined by repeat visits or content generated and uploaded.

Let's take a quick look at ways that a hypothetical small business can set clear marketing goals.

Let's assume the business sells gift baskets, has a small but loyal customer base, and wants to experiment with Facebook (by participating and spending £25 per day on hyper-local advertising). The small business could set the following goals for the first sixty days of its Facebook marketing efforts.

1. Get 50 new small customers.
2. Get 3 new larger customers (who order multiple gift-baskets).
3. Build brand awareness.

At the conclusion of the 60 day campaign, the business can evaluate the success or failure of that campaign by looking at the analytics and the important measurements. Did 50 or more new customers who were referred by Facebook order gift baskets? Did 3 or more new larger customers referred by Facebook place orders? Did the amount of email or messages from non-customers (referred by Facebook) asking questions about gift baskets increase over that month?

As you can see, the answer to each question is either a YES or NO. You either found 50 new customers through the Facebook campaign or you did not. You either found 3 new large customers or you did not. You either received more non-customer inquiries or you did not.

Now look at your own business and the marketing strategies and tactics that you are executing. Have you set clear goals for those strategies? If not, set aside some time this week and set clear goals – specifying

exactly what you hope to accomplish and in what
time-frame.

Chapter 3: Lean Marketing Things to Do for Your Brand

As the end of the year approaches, small businesses need to think not just about wrapping up the year that is fast coming to an end, but also towards planning and strategy for the new year. This planning can be on the micro end of the operational spectrum; budgeting, scheduling, and logistics, etc and it can also be on the grander, bolder, strategic end of the spectrum.

A good place to start is with your marketing strategy and for many small businesses this means a serious look at branding strategy. Lots of small businesses don't even have a branding strategy; they don't think this is for them, they think branding is for larger businesses and that small business and start-ups don't require a focus on branding. They also think that they don't have the budget to execute a branding strategy.

Wrong on both counts: Whether you are a brand new start-up trying to gain traction and visibility in the marketplace, or a local coffee shop or appliance repair business, your brand and your brand's presence in your market is what will provide you competitive advantage in both the short term and the long run. And for those of you who believe that branding requires a huge investment in media and advertising, you are probably thinking about this in the wrong way.

Many small businesses have turned to a DIY (Do It Yourself) approach to branding and have leveraged the social media as the foundation for their efforts. Social media is cheap, fast, flexible, powerful and, with an investment of sweat equity, can bring meaningful returns to a small business. Remember that branding does not have to be about universal recognition of your company, but rather about awareness within the market in which you are competing. Here is a list of 5 essential undertaking for any business seeking to leverage the social media in pursuit of brand awareness. None of these requires significant cash expenditure, but all require an investment of capacity, time, and human capital. Small businesses that commit to these practices will often see great results over time with the returns measured in traffic, revenue, customers, and word-of-mouth.

1. Listen!

This is probably the simplest thing you can do, but also the activity that requires the most commitment and attention. Right now; this very moment your brand and your competitors are being discussed somewhere by someone and it is critical that you are paying attention to what is being said.

Your company needs to be ready to respond, to answer questions, and to provide information to potential customers. Listening closely provides opportunity for growth, the occasion to improve, and the possibility to increase awareness through engagement. With a small investment of time, the data you can harvest also allows you to understand your company's "share of voice" in the social media and allow you to devise strategy and tactics for improvement.

Use the tools that the Internet provides you and make sure that someone from your company has their eyes and ears tuned in.

2. Get started

Start blogging, create Twitter profile for your business, build a Facebook page, start uploading video to YouTube, schedule a hangout on Google+... the very act of building your online presence in social media will have an impact. By reacting to, starting, and leading conversations online, you can attract followers and build reputation as a thought leader or establish your business as a source for subject-matter expertise. Remember that the goal is not just to attract people to interact with you (although this is critical) but rather that your conversations, posts, and other actions will take you beyond the first-degree dialog and intensify your presence and brand awareness.

3. Build culture

Your company may be too small for you to bother with creating specific social media "guidelines" or handbooks, but that doesn't mean you can't build a branding culture within your team. Encourage others to blog, to tweet, and to share content and ideas via your own social media pages. Your team can contribute to the branding by executing the same social media tactics and by leveraging their own audiences to build awareness and propagate ideas. Let each individual focus on their own area of expertise and passion; your developers can create a separate blog to discuss their own issues, challenges, and insights; your marketing team can engage with others on that specific aspect of business; and your finance whiz can provide information that will be of value to their own discrete audience, all in the service of brand-building.

4. Let it all hang out

Be transparent, be genuine, be honest, but mostly be ready to engage in honest and sincere conversations. Use the social media like geologists use remote sensors to predict seismic activity in other words by listening closely especially for negative comments experiences you have the opportunity to reach in a factual, legitimate and real way to the actual person on the other end of that tweet. By providing a personal, immediate response, you can build trust, create relationships, and engender positive feedback and word-of-mouth. People do love to complain loudly, but the opportunity to turn that person around can create an evangelist for your brand that money simply cannot buy.

5. Ask your customers

Many companies neglect the simplest, most straightforward, and possibly most effective tools for engaging customers and understanding how they feel about your company; ask! Put a poll out to your customers and ask them about themselves, who the are, where they live, what they do for a living; really anything you want to know is your for the asking. Better still conduct multiple polls with smaller slices of your customer base. Keep these short and be ready to offer an incentive to increase participation. Take the time and effort to curate content that you think will be valuable to your customers and your online audiences; by learning which types of content and which subjects are of interest, you can learn a great deal about your followers and your customers. Take the time to understand your audience and you can start to understand how and why they will buy your products, or use your services

Chapter 4: Lean Marketing Customer Service Strategies

Of the many things businesses can do well (or fail at) none is more important than customer service. Although the marketing textbooks, don't consider it to be one aspect of a solid marketing plan, this key function should be considered as a part of your marketing and approached the same way you would approach any of your other marketing tactics. I say this because the word of mouth that great customer service can engender is among the most powerful forces that can impact your business in a profound way improving revenues, strengthening margins, and increasing customer lifetime value all while reducing marketing expense in other areas, decreasing employee turnover, and leading to expanded visibility and awareness for your brand.

Great customer service does not have to be expensive, complicated, or slow. There are some wonderful tools available that can help you increase your customer service capacity, build an efficient infrastructure, and scale your ability to be responsive as your business grows. Here are some tips and tools which you can put to use as you learn to market through service.

1. Be available

Make yourself reachable by your customers in the ways they want to reach you. The best approach is to make yourself available to your customers in multiple ways: email support, phone support, instant chats are all tools that you can use. Of course this depends on your business and the resources you have available. For instance, many small companies simply do not have the capacity to offer full-time phone support, so many will offer it during certain specific hours. Chat is also a great way for customers to reach you, but this too may stretch your internal capacity. If you do offer these during limited hours, make sure to message this and be clear about exactly when you are available and by what means.

2. Be fast

Don't keep people waiting, whether it is for an answer to their email request or by simply limiting the hold time on your phone support. We are proud of the fact that 96% of all customer support requests that come in are answered in under one hour! But the flip to this is that you have to communicate how long it will take you to respond and to calibrate your customer's expectations to what you can realistically deliver; in other words, don't promise a response within 25 hours if you know it may take more than that.

3. Be honest

People appreciate transparency and your answer to their questions, comments, or suggestions are each an opportunity for you to establish an honest, open tone. This goes for everything from your message when they first contact you all the way through your answers to them when you are actually communicating. If your site is experiencing issues, tell them so; if you think a solution may take a long time, tell them that, too; and if you think their suggestion is one that is just not appropriate thank them and move on. They will appreciate the candour and will tell their colleagues how refreshing it is to deal with a company that tells the truth.

4. Be appropriate

Whether it's friendly and funny, or serious and business-like, the tone you adopt with your customers is critical in building a sustainable relationship. Listen to them and respond in kind. If a customer is angry about something, the last thing they want is to hear a snarky response and if they are being friendly and open, your tone should reflect the attitude they bring to your communication.

5. Be efficient

Scalability is critical in the way you look at your support structure and you should always bear this in mind as you make choices on how to deliver service. Your business is growing (hopefully really fast) and your support tools, staff, capabilities, and capacity need to be able to grow flexibly as your company scales. This doesn't mean that you need to add expensive capacity every week, but rather that you need to be smart in how you handle support and know when the time is right to ramp up resources and when finding additional efficiencies may be more appropriate. Among the things you could do to improve efficiencies are to develop great templates for answering often-asked questions, building admin tools to quickly solve common technical issues or extract relevant data for answers, adding and improving Help centre content and FAQs and making those easily available. In addition, you should iterated everything from your "Contact us" form to include tools to find answers to common questions and tweaked site content as well as email content to anticipate many user questions and common issues.

6. Be polite

When delivering support to your customers always pretends that your mom is in the room listening or reading over your shoulder. If your response passes her test for politeness then it's probably good. If mom would disapprove, well it's probably time to revise that answer or adjust that attitude, mister. Please remember to always apologize if your user is frustrated or angry and always, always be sure to say thank you. Right, mom?

7. Be thrifty

There is no reason that you need to spend massive amounts of money to deliver great service and support. Tools are readily available which can help you with your efficiency and capacity and technology can be leveraged to allow you to do more with less. Online resources abound, and these provide great features for collaboration, search, content updating, messaging, and automation. This is not to say that you shouldn't open the cheque book and hire that new customer service agent when the time is right, just that you should find creative ways of delivering service and support without spending piles of your hard-earned cash doing so.

Chapter 5: Lean Marketing Essentials for Customer Service

I had (another) bad customer service experience with an airline last week. I know a shocker. Sometimes I start to think that poor service and unhappy customers are a requirement for the airline industry. That this is a part of meeting some unwritten baseline needed for any entrant in the space. Then I come to my senses and remember that there are companies like Virgin who are competing in the industry, in part, by providing a high level of service; this company have, in turn, developed legions of fans and loyal customers.

Not surprisingly, my experience last week was with none of those wonderful operators, but rather with one of their old-line stodgy competitors, who I won't name. Ahhh, this airline has ancient fleet, the high fares, the grumpy flight attendants, and (apparently) the customer-phobic policies.

Without going into great detail, when returning last week from a wonderful conference, I asked this airline gate agent to help me with something. What I was requesting would not have cost a single dime in real or potential cost to them, would not have inconvenienced a single employee, and would not have impacted in any way any other customer. A few keystrokes would have accomplished my request and the net result would have saved me some hours of inconvenience and discomfort In other words a simple 'yes' to my request would have gone a great

27

distance towards making me a happy camper, and would even have earned them some kind and well-deserved word of mouth from me.

The airline's response was to tell me that they could indeed accommodate me, but that they would be charging me £275 to do so. When I lifted my jaw back off my chest, I asked the agent if they were kidding me. The answer was not surprising, "I am sorry, Mr. Asefeso, this is our policy and there is nothing we can do for you." Wow.

The experience started me thinking about how every day organizations miss simple opportunities to take an unhappy customer and turn them into a happy one. Just as important, organizations miss simple opportunities to avoid creating angry customers who can go around bad-mouthing a company. Why any company would not choose to create a potential evangelist for the brand is beyond me. It's that simple and, for me, it boils down to three simple rules to guide your interactions with customers:
1. Give them what they ask for,
2. Take the extra step for your customers, and
3. Learn from your interactions.

1. Give them what they ask for.

Seriously, why wouldn't you? If it is within your power to grant a request and the cost to your company is small or non-existent the default answer should always be a "yes." Your front-line team should always, always, always be trained and empowered such that it is as easy as possible for them to deliver this answer and they should always be ready to do so quickly.

Any time a customer, whether current, former, or potential, reaches out to you for help it is a unique occasion to engage that person, to learn from them, and to earn their loyalty. If they have taken the time to contact you, it should be viewed as an opportunity. Why? Because every company spends money to market to their audiences, to promote their brand, and to create an image. And nothing can do more to detract from that than an unhappy or angry customer. Of course, this is not possible in every single instance; sometimes satisfying the request may incur a real cost that may be too high to justify. Or sometimes, granting the request may mean inconveniencing another customer in some way. Simply put, the benefit to be gained by quickly and easily giving the customer what they asked for can be immeasurable. And, by corollary, the potential for creating an unhappy customer equally large.

2. Take the extra step.

Research has shown that brand loyalty is among the most powerful of forces in business. So, cultivating a loyal customer base pays off in many ways; for instance, word of mouth can be stimulated, the cost of acquiring new customers can be lowered, and repeat business can be improved upon. How do great companies do this? They go the extra step; they "surprise and delight," they do nice things for customers unbidden, and they anticipate their customer's needs as well as their pain points. And then, they attack; they find ways to provide extra value and not charge for it, they hand out goodies and rewards, and they constantly listen to their customers, analyze the data, and continuously improve their products or service to head off problems before they occur.

3. Learn from it.

When you have lots of different customers all making the same request of you, you probably are looking at an opportunity to improve. Why wait for yet another person to make the same request yet again? You need to constantly listen, consistently learn, and continually respond to what the customer wants. Capacity to learn and the celebration of learning itself, is a value that great companies share. If you can continuously learn from your customer's requests and from your customer's responses, your team will improve equally continuously and your customers will love you for it.

Chapter 6: Slice and Dice Your Customer Service Data

After every quarter I delve into our customer service data to have a look at a few things: first (and foremost) are we effectively meeting our goal of providing world-class customer service to our customers? Next, what is the demand on our system and do we have capacity available to meet it? Third, have we improved our performance across the key metrics of speed, quality, and efficiency?

We offer customer service through a number of channels: email, chat, social media, and phone and we collect and analyze the data from each of these channels. Email is, by far, our most important method for delivering service and over the past 3 years we have become adept at handling the volume as it has increased. The average time to respond to a new request via email has dropped from an average of almost 17 hours back in April of 2010 to an average of 4 hours last month; the time to answer a customer's question or resolve their issue (measured by the average "solve time," or the number of hours that a request is "open") has been reduced from almost 128 hours 3 years ago, to under 21 hours last month! In addition to increased capacity, we have also been able to consistently improve our performance through the use of customizable software tools, a clear understanding of the kinds of problems that typically arise, the ability to spot trending issues or problems, and the ongoing professional development of our team members.

The metrics I mention above are just that metrics. Of even greater importance to us is the quality of the support we deliver. Of course we have our share of angry and unhappy customers and we work very hard to help those folks. But the simple truth is that some folks will never be satisfied with the service your company can provide. But understanding your customer's perceptions of your service is critical. We track this in a number of ways, but the best way is also the simplest. When a support ticket is closed we always send that customer a very simple 1-question survey: "How was the quality of the customer support you received?" The survey is a way for us to get a snapshot of satisfaction at any given time. The satisfaction rating we received last month? 97% so far in April we are running at 99%! Our goal at all times is to push that number to 100%; we're still trying.

This chapter will focus specifically on our phone support channel. We started experimenting with phone support last year; first for Buyers only and on a limited number of pages. Initially we offered phone support for a limited number of hours per day and had one person who handled the small number of calls generated; as we got better at it and started implementing new tools, we slowly added more pages where the phone number was displayed and increased the number of hours it would be available. This past spring, we introduced the phone number site wide, made it available to all of our users, and increased the hours to 8am-6pm. The response has been overwhelmingly positive and we have quickly become adept at managing the process, training our agents, routing the calls, and handling an increasing volume of calls. We started using new software to help us with this and now our agents (many of whom work remote from HQ) answer incoming calls via laptop and headset anywhere they have an Internet connection.

We have collected the data on phone support for the past 2 quarters and have learned a great deal through the analysis of these numbers. We have adjusted our staffing to manage demand, we have developed protocols for handling different types of issue and customers, and we have tweaked everything from how calls are routed (i.e. which agent gets which call) to the music and messaging customers hear when they are on hold. But at the end of the day our analysis focuses on the same things we consider when analyzing data on email support. When do the calls come in?" "How many calls are there?" and "Are we improving?"

1. When?

With phone support, it is important to understand the day of the week and the time of day that customers call us. Answering phones can be exhausting work; customer problems, emotional outbursts, impatient users, and increasing volume can all add to the stress that a phone support agent must deal with. Scheduling is critical and this data allows us to schedule efficiently and effectively. In our case, we try to always have 2-3 agents handling calls during peak hours; this allows an agent to find some relief from the stress and assures that they are supported by the entire customer service team. In fact, all of our phone agents also handle email requests as well as chat sessions to relieve the pressure that comes with answering phones. These first two charts below show daily and hourly distribution of incoming calls, while the third shows how daily call volume has increased week-over-week since we started displaying our phone number across the site.

2. How Many?

Not just how many, but how long. As in minutes. Our agents have quickly learned that some folks just like to chit-chat, others have tons of questions, and still others need remedial training in basic computer skills. These customers necessarily talk longer and necessarily require greater capacity on our part. But knowing this informs our approach and helps us to deliver better service on the phone. For instance, we never limit the time needed to help a customer; a call can take 30 seconds or 30 minutes and our agents are trained to not rush callers. In fact, it is our policy to not set time limits on calls or even have targets. We do track the average call time for each of our agents, but not for performance review, but rather to get a feel for different styles of communication with our callers. Interestingly, there is very little difference on average call time between our agents who handle calls.

3. Are we improving?

This is difficult to measure empirically and we have identified some data which helps us to answer this question. One way to gauge improvement, and indeed to improve, is simply to listen. Eavesdropping (even though Mom told me it wasn't polite) provides a great opportunity for qualitative improvement when combined with meaningful review. Managers need to spend time observing phone support agents, listening critically, and providing ongoing feedback to help agents improve their skills and communication abilities. Beyond that, look at more empirical, quantitative data that might help. "How many calls go unanswered?" "How long is our average hold time?" "Is our capacity/coverage appropriate to the demand?" Answering questions like these, both empirical and subjective, can help you to find ways to constantly and consistently improve!

Chapter 7: Your Websites

Successful businesses know that to develop long-term relationships with their customers, they must find ways to build trust. This is not as easy to do as it sounds. According to the 2011 Edelman Trust Barometer study, U.S. consumer trust of companies dropped 8 points from 2010 to 2011.

In fact, this trend seems to be worsening. According to a new University of Melbourne study, online shoppers are 30% less loyal to online businesses than in 2007.

The good news is that businesses can improve their trustworthiness. The University of Melbourne study also found that Internet consumers are 20% more trusting of websites than they were five years ago. According to Dr. Brent Coker, the author of the study, the increase in online consumer trust is largely linked to the visual appeal of websites.

As aesthetically orientated humans, we are psychologically hardwired to trust beautiful people, and the same goes for websites. Our offline behaviour and inclinations translate to our online existence. As the internet has become prettier, we are venturing out, and becoming less loyal. With websites becoming increasingly attractive and including more trimmings, this creates a greater feeling of trustworthiness and professionalism in online consumers.

But it is not enough just to have a pretty website?

The biggest source of frustration is the inability to find relevant information on a website. The best way to stop defection to other websites, and increase loyalty, is to be interesting. Being pretty, but with nothing to say, is not enough.

Among other things, the University of Melbourne study found that if a website has poor navigation or access to information, or takes more than two seconds to download, prospective customers are more likely to opt against purchasing and navigate to another site.

Most companies, especially small business and start-ups are obsessed about the amount of traffic to their online sites. Site traffic is important; it brings attention, a certain degree of validation, and the opportunity to convert visitors into users or paying customers.

But traffic alone isn't enough and more importantly, we tend to overestimate its impact. Increased traffic can be "rich" with potential customers or simply pass-through traffic that never returns.

While obsessing over site traffic, many entrepreneurs short change their conversions strategy. This is a huge mistake. Make sure your site is ultimately monetized; you must understand how you can convert visitors into users or paying customers.

Chapter 8: Blogging to Build Audience and Drive Traffic

For many small businesses and start-ups, blogging is an inexpensive and effective strategy to drive traffic to a site, develop a reputation, and build an engaged audience of potential customers, even fanatics, who will share your content, promote your message, and help you to herd more readers to your site.

We have been publishing our blog since the day we launched our business and it has proven to be one of our more consistently successful strategies. A significant amount of the traffic to our site comes through the blog and many of our customers were first introduced to us by an article we posted that they somehow stumbled upon. We write for ourselves, but we also write with our audience of users in mind; small businesses, entrepreneurs, start-up folk, and creative types.

We blog because we are trying to build our business, but we also blog because we have things we like to share; topics that interest us, trends we become aware of, people we admire, and ideas we want to share. Here, then, are 5 tips on getting going with your own blogging strategy.

1. Start it up

There are tons of resources that allow you to set up your blog quickly and easily and many are free. First the question of self-hosting vs. Hosted has to be answered. Self-hosting carries great benefit, particularly if yours is a web-based business. Setting up a WordPress page or the like is a relatively simple process, but it does take time and energy to do so; the advantage is that when self-hosted your blog can act as a very effective portal and provides you with great control over design and functionality. The advantage of a hosted blog on a site like Tumblr, or Posterous is that you can have your blog up and running in minutes, leverage the built in communities those services offer, and allow you to focus solely on the content.

2. Focus

Pick a focus for your blog and work hard to make sure that 80% or more of your posts stay on target. For instance, the AA Global Sourcing Blog focuses on what we do and if you are a regular reader, you know that almost all of our posts are related to that topical area. More than anything, though, write with passion; readers want good writing and the best writing comes from the things you are most interested in that which moves and interests you. The posts your readers will find most compelling are also the posts that you cared the most about.

3. Be prolific

My number one rule for successful blogging: Produce. Set yourself a schedule and stick with it. Make a commitment to write a certain amount every week and then do so. If it is just you writing for the blog, you should probably try to write at least two articles a week. If multiple folks will contribute, one post per week is probably right. We have 4-5 folks writing for the blog regularly and others chip in a post periodically so in any given week we have 4-6 fresh articles; this steady stream of content is what readers look for and what keeps visitors returning.

4. Make it easy to share

Search is important when building an audience for your blog, but social media even more so. You need to spread the word and, more importantly, you need to make it easy for your readers to do so. Make sure that you make your posts easily linkable; share them on your Facebook, tweet them out to your follower, use a sharebar or other tool to make sharing a one-click proposition for your readers, and promote your posts via other pages on your site or in your email campaigns. The simpler it is for readers to share, the more they will.

5. Use the right words

Just not exclusively. Many bloggers are 100% focused on the SEO value that their blogs provide. While this is an important aspect (I mean, duh. If people can't find your blog through searches, then you might as well not bother) it should not be the only aspect. Take the time to figure out who your audience is and write for them, but also take the time to include words that they are searching for; one great (and free) resource is Google's Keyword Tool, which allows you to see which words the most people are searching for. If you

41

are an avid Vespa rider and you want to share your thoughts on the art of scootering with other enthusiasts, then write about that passion and they will find you.

Having said that, it doesn't mean that your posts and post titles should not include words that other scooter fans aren't searching for. In short, makes it easy for them to find you, but focus on what you want to say more so than making sure you use the right keywords.

Chapter 9: Giving Good Interview

In the world of start-ups and small business there are two basic kinds of company; those the media pays attention to, and all the rest. If your company has a compelling story, a unique product, or an interesting personality behind it you may be fortunate to leverage that advantage and convince a reporter to write about your offering, your customers, your employees, your industry, your background, your childhood, your pets… (you get the idea).

Most importantly, if the media does come knocking and asking questions, it is critical that you be prepared. Put together a media kit with appropriate background information; have persuasive pitches and story ideas at the ready; be facile with your facts and figures; and learn to make reporters comfortable that you are a credible and reliable source of information.

We often write about ways a company can create word-of-mouth and leverage buzz as inexpensive marketing techniques, and there is no better way to do this than to get your story placed or get yourself interviewed, People do read this stuff; they do remember what they read and they will spread the word if you give them the opportunity to do so. Here are 10 great tips shared with us by various PR and Media folks that I hope you find useful.

1. Prepare well

Before the interview make a short list of three or four points you want to make during the interview. Keep these simple and clear and keep the list in front of you so you can refer to it and keep the interview focused.

2. Stay focused

Concentrate on the interview and don't let anything distract you. If you are doing the interview on the phone, stay away from email and other potential interruptions.

3. Be in control

Make sure that the interviewer talks about the things you want to talk about. This doesn't mean that you shouldn't answer their questions, just that you should always find a way to move to your own message and your own agenda.

4. K.I.S.S

Pay close attention to the interviewer and their own interest in what you are saying; follow their lead on how technical and detailed to get in your answers but always keep it simple and clear. Short and memorable is way better than rambling and complicated, but keep the audience in mind as you craft your answers.

5. Be a credible source

Be yourself in these interviews and always remember that you have credibility or the journalist wouldn't be taking the time with you in the first place. Always be truthful and never misrepresent yourself or your company; it is your credibility on the line and even a minor fib can serve to destroy it.

6. Repeat yourself. Then reiterate

Remember that journalists take notes and if you can find a simple way to restate your main points at several junctures in the interview you have an even better chance that these will make it into the final piece. And after you have answered all the questions, recap the main points again.

7. Take your time

If a question catches you by surprise, give yourself some time to think by rephrasing the question or even repeating it. Never be afraid to ask the journalist to repeat the question if you need a moment to consider your answer.

8. Give great sound bites

Keep in mind three things:
1. Your major selling point or what you are there to talk about.
2. The proof behind your selling point.
3. Making the journalist and their audience care about what you have to say.

Great politicians are masters at this, they understand well how to make a point, back it up, and illustrate it so that the audience can relate. This is your challenge and your goal in every interview.

9. Handle them before they handle you

Answering questions is an art and you should be prepared to handle the difficult ones as well as the easy ones. Don't avoid the hard questions; be prepared for these and use them to bridge back to your own key message. Try not to repeat back negative language or ideas, just calmly assert your own position and get your point across without actually acknowledging the negative point.

10. Watch what you say

If you don't want to see it in the media, then don't say it! Remember they will write what you say and the information will come from you first. Better to bite your tongue than to get bit when the interview is published.

Chapter 10: Lean Marketing Public Relations Strategies

One of the least expensive and most effective ways that small businesses can grow is through the strategic application of public relations. PR can be executed on a modest budget, and the awareness and word-of-mouth that can be attained is priceless for a small company.

PR is typically a mix of social media, community participation, public speaking opportunities (including appearances at trade shows and conferences), media commentary, and long-term relationships with reporters (both local and national) leading to press and online coverage.

There are dozens of inexpensive PR tactics and resources that small companies can leverage, and in this chapter we will explore a few best practices, DIY approaches, and valuable strategies that small businesses can leverage to great effect.

Setting goals for your company is critical in your approach to PR. You should determine exactly what it is you are trying to accomplish through public relations efforts and then measure your progress towards that goal. Want 3 national press mentions in the next 12 months? Inclusion in 15 local media stories? 2,500 Twitter followers? Determine exactly what you want to accomplish and measure your progress against those goals. If the tactics you are executing are working, great. If not, be ready to move on to the next one; try lots of different ideas and, as in all aspects of your business, don't be afraid to fail. Here are some tips and resources that we leverage, utilize, or otherwise live by in our own PR efforts:

Know your audience

It is critically important that you understand your audience, whether these are your own customers (or potential customers), magazine writers, academics, or influencers of other stripes. Take the time to understand who you are trying to reach and target your efforts towards them. For instance, if your customer base is accountants and your geographical strategy is national, take the time to identify the journals accountants subscribe to, the conferences they attend, and the blogs they read. When you have a good picture of how they consume information and the information they need, you can strategically target your message and tailor your content for them.

Create a budget

Like most small businesses, you are probably working with limited resources and while PR is important, you may not have much of a marketing budget to work with. Determine for yourself how much you can spend over a given period of time and prioritize how you will do so. Fortunately many of the resources we discuss here are free and much of the work can be done by you, so save up the funds for swag, meals and contests that may require modest outlay of real cash.

Have a plan

Without a PR plan, these tactics can be disconnected from a larger strategy and will not return the results you are looking for. Set goals and then "back into" those goals with solid strategy and concrete tactics designed to reach them. Set up a calendar and be disciplined about sticking with it; you might consider a monthly "focus" such as geographical, industry, or even media outlet. Create lists of reporters, blogs, and Twitter users that you will target and use these lists to support your strategy and stick to your calendar.

Be consistent

Be special. Have a personality. The idea is to make yourself a resource that others will rely on. If you are an auto mechanic, make sure everyone knows that you are the go-to source for information on everything automotive. Set yourself apart as the "funny" mechanic, or the "socially conscious" mechanic; make sure they remember you and not the other guy down the street. Finally, have a personality and don't be shy about using it, we tend to listen to those who interest us, and often that interest is based not just on knowledge on a given subject, but in the way it is presented and the language that is used.

Leverage others

Identify thought leaders and help them to know and love your brand. Follow key users on Twitter to get a better sense of their personality and interests; re-tweet them, engage them, and develop relationships over time. Get them engaged with you (and your brand); the goal is to get them to talk about you with their own audiences whether it is because they have used your product or service or because they simply like the things you have to say.

Share

Be an active part of the dialogue and do so by creating content that in turn you contribute to the wider community. Developing partnerships with other businesses to reach their customers offer them something that they can give to their own customers whether it's a discount for your services or products or an article for their newsletter. Read other businesses blogs and comment on them; tweet great links and follow others on Twitter who do the same. Get your entire team tweeting, so as to reach a broader audience. And don't just talk about your business, but talk instead about how you can solve problems for your customers.

Pitch like a major leaguer

Don't be afraid to pitch reporters; the stories that people like you bring to them are the life blood of any media outlet. Writers and editors are always looking for great story ideas and as long as your pitch is timely and on topic, they will listen. And just because they don't bite on your current pitch, don't give up, you should focus on developing the relationship by asking questions, giving and getting real-time feedback, and developing a one-on-one relationship which allows you to share useful information and give that writer the benefit of your own perspective and personality. Remember to keep your pitches simple; if written, keep them to one page or less, plus make sure your pitch is relevant to the writer's own area of concentration. Finally, be sure to follow up; these are busy people and just because they didn't respond immediately, doesn't mean they might not be interested; just don't be annoying or obnoxious and make sure you are always polite and respectful.

Folks do like gifts. Don't try to understand why, but people love trinkets, pens, buttons, stickers, toys, mugs, hats for whatever reason, human beings just gobble up whatever it is you are giving away. Oh yea remember to put your company name and logo on whatever swag you are handing out this week otherwise it misses the entire point.

Know your resources

There are dozens of free and cheap tools available to get the word out, build awareness, and interact with customers. For your press releases there are tons of free sites on which to post:
1. PRWeb
2. Free Press Release
3. PRLog

The above are a few of the many available. HARO (help-a-reporter-out, get it?) is a go-to resource for PR professionals as well as reporters; when a writer need sources for an upcoming story, they post on HARO seeking people who can help; when a businessperson wants to position him or herself as a subject-matter expert they too can post on HARO listing themselves as a source for stories or information. PR gold.

Be a resource

Create content designed to position yourself an indispensable authority on your industry, your city, your profession or any appropriate topic. Create and make available case studies to provide valuable information to the media and your customers. Position yourself as an expert by writing white papers to distribute to your readers and other professionals. Blog on a topic you know well and engage with your readers in the comments section of your blog. When you create great content, opportunities will present themselves; for instance, many trade publications will publish those case studies, and lots of other blogs will want to re-publish your pieces. The more places you can post your content the greater the effect it can have; use YouTube for the videos you create, Flickr for the photos you take, and your Facebook fan page for everything and anything. If a resource exists, use it!

Share your resources

Lastly, become a resource for others by making information easily available: set up an online press centre; compile all of the stories, mentions, and press releases you have generated and make them easily accessible. Be sure to include a downloadable press kit with information on your company, your team, and your service or product as well as photos, bios, and any other material that will be helpful for those who want to write about you.

Most start-up entrepreneurs and marketing professionals will agree that a robust public relations strategy is crucial for start-ups and many small businesses. While there is no argument that these efforts can provide great value in the form of awareness, traffic, word of mouth, and brand positioning, the efficacy of PR is, at best, difficult to measure.

For online businesses in particular, marketing tactics can and should be measurable and a positive ROI is an indicator that a given stratagem is working. If a £1 investment in marketing returns of £1.50 then it is a good bet that most entrepreneurs will continue to invest in a particular tactic. On the other hand, a tactic that costs the same £1 but returns just 75p would be a target for early termination.

With some marketing efforts ROI success is remarkably simple to analyze; for instance, paid search is easily tracked, the resulting data is readily available, and arriving at a CPA is a virtual no-brainer. PR is different; in most cases there is little reliable tracking data available, your ability to correlate customer traffic to PR placements is dubious, and your PR spend often falls into 'leap-of-faith' territory. Many companies, however, are ready to act on that faith; the portion of the budget they devote to PR must be viewed as an investment in raising brand awareness, positioning the company in the marketplace, or establishing industry leadership.

Media coverage brings credibility and part of establishing a start-up or young company is to develop and leverage that credibility. As a company matures, continuing press coverage helps to sustain brand awareness and positioning and to boost momentum as growth continues.

There are several things for small businesses to keep in mind when assessing the success of a PR program or considering an investment in one. Here are four thoughts to keep in mind as you manage your PR efforts:

1. Focus

When crafting a PR plan, focus is critical to its success. Focus on the message you wish to convey, the audience you wish to reach, and the types of media you hope to receive coverage in. Set goals for the number of placements you would like to receive over a given period, the number of impressions you wish to accumulate, and the capacity you are willing to devote. Determine for yourself 'tiers' of media that are important to you. For example you might wish to focus on media outlets that have very large circulation, or outlets that provide a valuable target audience. Take the time to define your own tiers and then determine how much of your capacity will be devoted to earning placements in each of those.

2. Target

The audience you are targeting should define where you want coverage and what you want the coverage to be about. Keep in mind that some outlets will be better for your company than others and that reputation counts; everyone knows the New York Time, The Wall Street Journal, and Forbes Magazine and any of us would be happy to have our companies covered in the pages of those august publications. But there are literally thousands of media outlets, industry publications, radio shows, blogs, and newsletters available that can help you to reach the right audience. Remember that placement is a game of impressions and while those impressions in aggregate can have a real impact, sometimes it is the quality of the eyeballs themselves that can determine the success of your PR plan.

3. Track

Determine from the start what exactly you will measure and the metrics for doing so. Using the 'tiers' strategy is one way to measure, harvesting raw numbers such as impressions or circulation is another. In fact, while CPM is not typically a metric that we use when determining marketing success it is one of the few harvestable pieces of data that a PR plan can generate. Our approach is to discount the data conservatively for instance, if a given platform publishes traffic data our process would be to cut that number by 50% or more to arrive at our own estimate of reach and impact. Public relations professionals often look at other ratios and measurements including Advertising Value Equivalency (AVE) and other PR Multipliers.

4. Build

PR professionals will tell you, correctly, that this is an industry built on relationships and build those, you must. Media professionals, journalists, bloggers and others will typically turn to people they know and sources they consider reliable when looking for opinions, quotes, or expert analysis. There is a symbiotic relationship that exists between these professionals and they are uniquely dependent on one another. PR professionals cannot be successful without placements and media professionals are reliant on the PR folk for leads, story ideas, and background material. Entrepreneurs can and should develop ongoing relationships with writers and others who can help their companies and whom they can also help when called upon.

Chapter 11: Increasing Lifetime Value With Email Campaigns

It is a truism of the business world that it costs more to acquire a new customer than it does to retain an existing one. It is also a truism that every business extracts a relatively predictable economic value from a given customer based on amount of money spent with a company minus the amount of money it cost to acquire that customer. A company that can focus on successfully increasing this 'customer lifetime value' (CLV) by providing ongoing value to customers and nurturing the relationship can meaningfully improve its bottom line profitability.

Having said that, wow do I hate receiving junk in my work email? Like most of us, I have multiple email accounts: work, personal, personal number two, and junk. My junk email is an account I use specifically to sign up for random websites, to conduct ecommerce, and to avoid the mailing lists that my accounts inevitably (and magically) appear on. This doesn't mean that various newsletters, marketing campaigns, and other communications don't slip into my work email, it just means that I try hard to limit those and will not hesitate to clink 'unsubscribe' when necessary. But there are still many lists from which I do not unsubscribe. These are the ones that don't just market to me, but the ones that also provide me with something more; knowledge or entertainment or ideas that I deem worthy of consumption. A company that can keep my attention is also a company whose marketing message I am much more likely to accept and act upon if I believe the value is good.

A great example of this for me is a company based here in London, Homemade Pizza Company. This is a great chain of takeout pizza stores that sells, high-quality, and fresh, gourmet pizzas that you cook at home in the oven or on the grill. They have a great product and a great marketing team. I probably receive 1 or 2 of their emails a week and I allow them to continue sending to me because;

1. I like their product.
2. Their emails are always colourful and attractive with great written content and pretty photos of yummy pizza.
3. They often provide me with tips and ideas for preparing meals (I like to cook).
4. The emails often come with coupons or other discounts that I can take advantage of.

In short, Homemade Pizza has succeeded in holding my interest, building a relationship with me, and increasing my CLV by encouraging me to come back and buy another pizza (or a salad they also make great salads).

Email campaigns specifically targeted at an existing customer base take careful strategy, artful tactical execution, an awareness of audience and messaging, and careful analysis in order to be successful. Here are 5 best practices to consider as you launch your own email campaigns.

1. Know your audience

A meaningful understanding of your customer base is critical to success in email campaigns. The Homemade Pizza Company knows me well enough to guess that I am interested in food and cooking, that high quality, fresh ingredients are important to me, and that I am a sucker for pretty photos of great looking food. The content they provide in their mailings is rich in those things, so HPC is providing me value when they show up in my inbox. They are also smart enough to understand the 'cookie' strategy; in other words along with the valuable content they send me the occasional sweet goodie in the form of a coupon or discount offering. It's like finding the prize in the box of crackerjacks and I probably redeem 25-50% f the offers they send. (Which is a phenomenal rate of redemption in the universe of online marketing.)

2. Target and segment

Pick and choose among your customers as you design your campaigns. If you have a reasonably large list it is to your advantage to segment and target carefully within that list. Remember that not every customer is alike and what one finds valuable another might find useless. We tend to send offers out regularly, but they are typically sent to a smaller slice of our base rather than the entire list. For instance one week we might send something out only to new customers who have registered on the site in the past 6 months. Alternately we might send a mailing to 'power' buyers who have posted 10 or more projects with us over the years. We probably have 10 active segments going at any given time and we constantly look for new segments to target as long as we think that we can give them something that will be of value to them.

3. Subject line is critical

Keep subject lines short and to the point (under 50 characters is a good rule) and make them compelling; creating some sense of urgency is important. The goal of the subject line is to increase your "open rate," or the percentage of recipients who actually view your email. Your subject line should grab attention and serve as a call to action, so offering a discount or other freebie directly in the subject line can sometimes make a big difference and can incentivize readers to open and read your mailing: "£5 off today!" "But on pizza, get the second for free!" It is also a great idea to test different subject lines to see which is more effective; most email providers offer this feature and will allow you to split your list in order to try out different subject lines to compare results in open rates, click through, and conversions. Keep careful track of which work best and stick with the winners.

4. Recognize the risk

Because there will always be someone on your list who really doesn't want your emails, there will always be unsubscribes, opt-outs, and complaints. This means that every time you send a mass email to your customers you are taking a risk that you will lose some or that you may even be reported for spamming. These actions have a real impact: a lost customer represents an overall decrease in CLV, and spam reports (if enough of them are generated) can sometimes result in an ISP (Internet Service Provider) blocking your emails from all of their users. You can imagine the impact on your mailing list of Yahoo put you on its blacklist, right? It is important that you track this data; keep a sharp eye on the percentage of recipients who unsubscribe and the number of spam complaints your emails receive. If either of these are increasing you have a problem, and should look very carefully at your overall strategy, including timing, targeting, and content.

5. Track it

Every email provider offers told for reporting and analysis of your mail campaigns. Mailchimp (which we use for our newsletters and marketing campaigns) provides simple and powerful reporting which, among other things, allows us to track each campaign individually, compare to past campaigns, a/b test subject lines, and experiment with sending campaigns on different days of the week as well as times of day to track the results.

Remember that many people HATE email and view your marketing messages as spam. You have to know your customers and respect your audience and if this means leaving them alone, then do so.

Chapter 12: Hyperlocal Marketing Channels

We talk often about marketing strategies and tactics for small business and start-ups. These companies typically have limited budgets, thin resources, and strained capacity which combine to create a challenge for managers and owners; how to develop an effective marketing campaign using tactics that will work for their business.

The Lean Start-up movement provides a wonderful template, on how managers can use these principles in their own marketing campaigns. We have written about many tactics that have worked in our own marketing efforts, such as public relations, goal-setting, branding, etc.

In this chapter we want to focus on tactics with a local flavour. A phrase we hear a great deal is "hyperlocal," which Wikipedia defines as being "synonymous with the combined use of mobile applications and GPS technology." I would enlarge that scope beyond mobile applications and GPS, and explain hyperlocal marketing as a strategy for reaching a specific, targeted audience located in a very specific geographical location. In other words, hyperlocal is a way for marketers to deliver an effective marketing message to customers in a particular local community.

This is nothing new for marketers; a great example of hyperlocal marketing that has been with us for decades is the Yellow Pages. This still ubiquitous book of business listings, made of the cheapest paper stock available and found on shelves and in recycling bins everywhere, has historically been a great way for businesses to reach local customers from "AAAA Auto Repair" all the way down to "ZZZZ Welding." But the world of marketing has grown way more sophisticated, and in the age of GPS and QR codes, small business can leverage some sophisticated tactics to reach local audiences, build awareness neighbourhood by neighbourhood, and make the most of a limited marketing budget. Here are 5 ideas for hyperlocal marketing that you can consider for your own business:

1. Yellow pages

If it still works and still fits your budget, why not experiment with this chestnut? For very small sums a business can target a very specific local audience (in many cases right down to the post-code). If nothing else, using Yellow Page advertising guarantees that your business name is right there along with your competitions and that you have an equally good chance of capturing the customer who is looking for you. Most of the Yellow Page publishers now include online listings along with the print version, which can also serve to enhance a business's web presence and SEO efforts.

2. Daily deals

Groupon, Living Social, Woot, and the like are available in virtually every city in the US and many more cities in Europe. For lots of businesses, particularly brick and mortar, these services offer a way to reach a very large audience of potential customers and pay only for those that actually show up to buy. The downside is that many of the folks who actually buy these deals are fickle and may never return once they have used their coupon with you. The upside is that this tactic can be a great way to build your customer base and to get your brand in front of millions of potential customers at a relatively modest cost.

3. Mobile

Alright, here is where that mobile and GPS thing comes in. Applications such as Foursquare, Yelp, and Urbanspoon allow businesses to build awareness and reputation online. I don't know about you, but when I travel Yelp is a go-to app for me; I need a good place for breakfast near my hotel and I log in and do a quick search. Restaurants near my location pop up complete with photos and reviews and before I know it, there I am sipping coffee and eating eggs with bacon. Yum yum yum and huge value delivered to that restaurant and to me the customer. Foursquare does that but also allows businesses to offer their own coupons and discounts available to anyone who stops by and checks in. Bacon and eggs taste even better when they come with a nice discount, no? In addition, social media platforms such as Facebook and Google+ allow local targeting of online ads. For the marketer, the cost of these tactics is small and the ability to track ROMI in real-time is powerful.

4. Outdoor and print

QR code marketing has brought outdoor advertising into the 21st century by tying together the ancient art of cave painting with the modern art of website metrics. Customers love having the ability to learn more about a company or a product or a house for sale simply by pointing their smart phone at a sign or a poster and learning more right there on the spot. Marketers get the reach they crave via outdoor advertising on billboards, bus kiosks, and telephone pole handbills and at the same time get the ability to track analyze real data and real sales. Print ads in magazines as well as door hangers and mail stuffers can also include QR codes and marketers add transparent value to these time-tested tactics.

5. Direct mail

For 14.5¢ businesses can use the Every Door Direct Mail service to reach out directly to potential customers via the United States Post Office and target these customers right down to specific mailing routes; the same applies in the UK and major European countries. Marketers can search for zip codes in their city (or nationally) that match the demographics they are working to reach; and with targeted mailing routes you can send direct mailings in batches as small as a few dozen or as large as 5,000! The United States Post Office has a great demo tool which allows you to play with targeting zip codes, routes and customer types that gives you a real time cost.

Chapter 13: Facebook Advertising

We write often of low-cost, high impact marketing tactics for small businesses and share tips for leveraging these. We believe that small business and start-ups should always be willing to experiment with marketing tactics and strategies as long as those serve a larger goal and contribute to a clear strategy.

The key to this approach is to set very specific incremental goals, carefully collect and analyze the resulting data, and be ready to do one of two things based on what the data tell you. If the results are positive, repeat and iterate that tactical experiment as long as it is moving you towards the defined goal. Alternately, if the tactic is failing, be ready to quickly terminate the experiment.

Search engine marketing is a tactic that is perfect for a lean, iterative approach to marketing. Paid search allows small business owners to easily set simple, reasoned goals and then, based on the data collected, make adjustments and decisions rationally. For instance, if you have a simple goal of driving additional traffic to your site it is easy to measure the results (and cost) of the SEM campaign. Define for yourself exactly how much traffic you wish to result from the tactic, and how much money you are willing to spend for the additional traffic. The resulting data will tell you quickly whether you have accomplished that goal.

We have provided advice on using Google Adwords as well as other platforms, in this chapter I want to share some advice on best practices for using Facebook as an advertising platform. Facebook advertising's greatest benefit is the network effect. If a Facebook user interacts with your ad by 'Liking' it, that 'Like' is automatically shared with the user's entire network of FB friends. This is a powerful magnifier, not just in terms of the word-of-mouth amplification that brings your message to many more people, but because of the 'endorsement effect' that accompanies the word-of-mouth. Studies have indicated that as many as 90% of consumers are more likely to trust recommendations from people they know. In other words, we all take advice from our friends and if one of them 'Likes' a certain FB ad, then we are more inclined to try that product or service ourselves.

Here is a short tutorial for getting your Facebook campaign going:

Set goals

Be very clear with what you are trying to accomplish with your Facebook campaign. Is it to gain fans for your business's FB page? To drive traffic to your own site? To generate sales and revenue? It is crucial that goal definition include conversion definition. For instance is a visit to your site what you would consider a conversion? Is a user registration or harvested email address a conversion? Or does it have to be an actual sale for you to consider it a conversion? Define what a conversion is and be clear on how much you are willing to pay for each conversion. The only way to measure the campaign's success is to articulate for yourself how you define success and to measure the data against that definition.

Target effectively

Facebook allows you to target your ads to very specific segments and demographics. You can segment by a user's location, language, or by the industry the user works in. Alternatively you can target by personal demographics like age, relationship status, education or even by birthday. For instance you could target your ads only at people in California, who are single, and whose birthday it is today. You could even choose to target only people who is 37th birthday is today. This ability to slice and dice by the audience you want, and not just be those searching for specific words or terms can be incredibly powerful.

Determine ad type. You will have to choose between two approaches with your Facebook ads; CPC or CPM. CPC is the cost-per-click model and with this you will only pay for the actual click-throughs that your campaign generates. With CPM (or cost-per-thousand views), you are paying for the number of impressions, or actual people, that see your ad appear on a FB page they visit. This choice should be driven by your own goals; if the objective of the campaign is to drive traffic to your site, then CPC will be a more measurable choice. If, alternatively, you are trying to raise awareness of your brand or service, then a CPM approach might make more sense.

Budgeting, bidding, and structures

Like AdWords, Facebook allows the advertiser to set a daily budget which is not to be exceeded. For instance, you may determine that your daily limit will be £200 and that (using the CPC ad type) you will pay as much as 50p per click. At this threshold you will receive a minimum of 400 clicks before your budget for the day is depleted. Remember though, as with AdWords, you are competing with other advertisers to get your ad in front of the intended audience and this is where bidding comes in. You will need to determine not just a daily budget, but the maximum amount that you are willing to pay for each click (or for each thousand views with a CPM approach). So if you set your bid at that 50p per click maximum, your ad will be less likely to run than your competitor's who may be offering 60p per click. Think not just budgetary, but strategically and remember to let your own goals, and your own business economics drive your bidding strategy.

Test your ads

A/B testing. or champion/challenger testing is an important way to understand what works for your intended audience and what doesn't. This can be as simple as testing alternative headlines, images, or body content. When you run two ads head-to-head, it can quickly be determined which is more effective in reaching your stated goal and maximizing your budget. Other testing strategies include testing your ads at different times of day, testing against different segments or demographics, and testing different bids. Any of these tests will give you valuable data and allow for iteration and experimentation.

Finally, create lots of ads. Everyday try new ads, with new copy and new images. Every day target a new segment with a new message; then stick with the ones that are working, and quickly kill those that aren't.

Make them Like you

One of the more common strategies with FB ads is the use of a 'reveal tab'. This technique displays a special offer or download available to the user, only if they Like your ad or your page. By giving a FB user a reason to Like your ad, such as a free download, a discount coupon, or other value which will be provided to them only if they click the Like button. The old rule applies here; to get something, you have to give something.

Analyze and iterate

Then analyze and iterate again. In the tips above, I talked about setting goals, targeting, bidding, budgeting, and testing. The most important point is what you do with this information. It's pretty simple: collect the data, analyze the data, and then act on the data. For instance if you test against various target segment, take the time to scrutinize the data, and adjust your ads based on which segment responds to your ads more often. Iterate based on this information and adjust your targeting accordingly. If your testing reveals that one image results in more Likes than another, then focus your ads on the image that is converting more effectively. This constant cycle of test, iterate, test again will allow you to refund your campaign and make the most effective use of your budget.

Give it time

Facebook advertising takes time. Not just the time to test different approaches, ad types, target segments, and bids, but time in the sense of capacity. It is critical that you carefully and deliberately track your campaigns, adjust your approach, and measure your progress. Doing this takes precious hours, and as small business owners and managers, we all know that these hours are our most valuable commodity. Budget your resources as well as your money, and remember that the two go hand-in-hand; to get the most from your money, be sure to devote the time needed to do the job right.

Chapter 14: Business Card As Selling Tool

Just about everybody has one. Your desk has probably is littered with little piles of them. I would be willing to bet good money, that right now you have a few of your own in your wallet or purse. In the past year you have probably handed out and received literally hundreds of these tiny leaflets; an ongoing marketing effort that we don't often think of as marketing.

Small businesses can spend tens of thousands of dollars with direct marketing efforts that might include mailers, trade show handouts, brochures, door-hangers, coupons, product spec sheets and more. But what we don't do is treat that little 2"x3.5" slip of paper with our name and contact info as what it is; the best opportunity you have to market yourself or your business to a truly targeted and captive audience; the person to whom you hand it.

It is time to think of your business card as not just a handy way to share your email address, but as a selling opportunity. Approach the design and content of your business card differently; stop right now to consider what other messaging, information, or purpose your card might include.

Here are seven ways you can leverage those tiny slips of paper to spread the word, stand out from the crowd, and make the most of each and every opportunity to market your company.

1. Multitask

Your business card can serve purposes other than just sharing your info. Creative business people are using theirs to offer discounts, include coupons, serve as event tickets, note cards, or appointment cards. Clever and fun uses like scratch cards or stickers can be memorable and can encourage the recipient to hold onto that card and jog their memory about you at an opportune moment.

2. Drill-down

Your card can include your own QR code or SKU and can encourage the other person to come have a look at your site. This way potential leads can view additional information or even receive discounts or other incentives. This is also a great way to track the efficacy of the card you will know that every user who comes to the URL via that code was someone whom you met at a given event. Not a bad way to measure conversions of a very different sort.

3. Testify

Another great marketing strategy is to show a potential customer how others like them have benefitted by using your product or service. We do this in other marketing materials; why not use the back of your business card for a short testimonial from a happy customer? Quotes, photos, and links can help to illustrate how others have used your business successfully and can provide the confirmation that a potential customer needs.

4. Educate

Use your card to teach them something. Little facts, statistics, or other information can make your card fun, engaging and memorable. Think about how much fun those little Trivial Pursuit cards are and how you can get a bit of that going with yours!

5. Fundraise

Business cards can have a more meaningful life than just sharing your digits. I have seen cards from several folks that promote something more than just their own business, but also provide information about a favoured cause or charity. Good feelings are remembered, and selfless acts admired. Let the person you hand your card to know that you are passionate and caring and they will be more likely to dig out your card when they are ready to buy.

6. Network

The exchanging of business cards is probably the most effective networking method there is. Your challenge is to make your card sticky and give it the best chance of converting a prospect into a customer.

One effective tactic is to include your photo on your card; this is a great way to help someone remember you as a person. Encourage or even incentivize others to hand out your card for you.

7. Incentivize

What if you gave each person you meet 5 cards, each with a coupon code? Tell the recipient that if all five coupons are redeemed, they too will receive a discount or something else of value. Heck, if they hand out 100 cards for you, give them a television set! Finally, perhaps it is time for you to be the first on your block to embed a GPS chip in your biz card so you can track how far it travels. Hey if your pet can have one, why not your biz card?

Chapter 15: Which Type is Your Brand?

Building and managing your brand, its identity, its name, and its reputation is critical to your company's ultimate success. How (and when and where) you connect with your customers is determined in large part by your branding and by how your audience relates to your brand. Markets are more competitive than ever, and the quality of products and services are more consistent so, in many cases, your branding will become your strongest differentiator in the marketplace.

In this chapter I would like to discuss the three types of brands, what distinguishes each, and some thoughts on how this can help you to determine the optimal marketing mix of strategy and tactics.

1. Functional brands

A functional brand is typically bought to satisfy a functional need on the part of the consumer. Automobiles, cell phones, and dish soap are examples of functional brands. Functional brands are tied in the consumer's mind to specific product categories and typically share the user's associations with other brands in the same category. For instance, all automobiles share in their basic functionality; they are designed to transport passengers from point A to point B and they all do the same thing in essentially the same manner. Because of this, functional brands must differentiate from their competitor's brands by stressing either better performance or better economy.

1. **Performance:** BMW is an automobile brand that maintains category leadership by spending heavily on product research and design to produce cars that are faster, more luxurious, and with greater cutting edge design relative to the competition. BMW cars are known for their sophisticated and elegant styling as well as their high-performance components and when BMW launches a new model; it is positioned based on these qualities and BMWs marketing.

2. **Economy:** Kia is a South Korean automobile company which also produces many models sold in the US and around the world, but this company competes based on perceived economic value. Kia also spends a great deal of money on R&D, but the focus is on finding ways to reduce cost through increased manufacturing efficiency, simpler design, and more modest features. Kia has become a leader in the market, based on their ability to introduce products at a price point that is attractive to many automobile buyers. Kia competes by striving to produce a high-quality car at a low price.

Building and managing a functional brand is dependent on focusing the marketing mix on either the product itself (for superior performance) or on place and price (for superior economy). Advertising and messaging must support the connection between the brand and the category; but must also stress what it is that makes the brand superior, either in functionality and features, or in price and overall value.

2. Image brands

Image brands create value by building specific perception in user's minds. Certain fashion, food, and liquor products are image brands and they differentiate themselves because buyers perceive them as offering a unique association or image. For instance, while clothing is typically a functional product, many huh-end fashion brands are marketed based on the image used to differentiate it from the competition.

1. **Feature-based:** Many image brands create their image based on product features. A good example of this is the Mazda Miata sports car. This car was designed to evoke the features and feel of the classic British roadster; top down, and that great sense of speed when driving. In addition, Mazda designed in features ranging from a special speedometer to a specialized exhaust system which evokes the sound of the classic sports cards from MG and Triumph.

2. **User Imagery:** Ralph Lauren is a clothing brand that is built on images of exclusivity, high style, and luxury. Lauren uses imagery of country estates, antique cars, and beautiful models to impress upon consumers the

exclusive nature of the product and the Advertising. Many image brands use advertising specifically to create associations that are not dependent upon features. Great examples of this are the Marlboro Man in tobacco advertising and the current ads for Dos Equis beer. Both of these brands use an actor to convey an image of individualism and rugged adventure, one through images of the old west and the other with humorous ads extolling the virtues of "the most interesting man in the world."

Managing an image brand is a function of creating an emotional connection with the customer. Image brands depend on their ability to tap into consumer's desires to belong to a social group, or to be admired by others, or to define themselves according to a particular image. Because of this, advertising plays a huge role in building these brands, as well as other forms of communication such as sponsorships and publicity.

3. Experiential brands

Experiential brands differ from image brands in one important respect; where image brands focus on what the product represents; experiential brands are all about how the product makers the users feel when interacting with the brand. An experiential brand is not always a tangible product, but in many cases is a place or a service which delivers a sensory experience or encounter with the brand. Starbucks is an experiential brand; while the product is coffee and other beverages and food items, the real product is the experience of the store itself. Comfortable seeing, stylish design, WiFi connectivity, work space, and music are all part of the experience the brand provides. Another example of an experiential design is Six Flags amusement parks. Here a consumer pays admission in exchange for the thrills and adrenaline-inducing rides available in the park.

The dimensions of an experiential brand are primarily its potency (intense or mild) and its activity (passive or active). Most experiential brands deliver a positive experience (think Disney or Elizabeth Arden salons) but vary in the intensity of the experience as well as the activity involved. Disney theme parks, while varying in intensity are, for the most part, active experiences, while Elizabeth Arden provides as mild and passive experience.

Managing experiential brands are primarily a challenge of consistency. Starbucks takes great care when hiring and training employees to assure a good cultural fit and the ability to convey the brand values and deliver on the brand experience. Disney, too, is known for the care it takes in hiring, training, and managing employees, as well as maintaining the spotless and cheerful atmosphere of the parks.

Chapter 16: Lean Marketing for Not-for-Profit

Like small businesses, most not-for-profits have limited resources, ambitious goals, and finite capacity. Many NFPs operate in ways that would not be considered 'business-like, and these organizations, like their small, for-profit cousins, can benefit by leveraging the ideas and tools of Lean Marketing.

Here are 8 tips for not-for-profit organizations on marketing their organizations, and some tools and suggestions for setting goals, maximizing resources, and extending capacity.

1. Define your goals

Many NFPs have long-range plans, ambitions, and a clear mission. But one of the tenets of lean marketing is to define short-term and intermediate goals. It is of critical importance that NFPs define smaller, intermediate goals which are highly measurable and allow the organization to assess whether the strategies and tactics in use are successful. When determining these it is important to be as specific as possible, and to determine in advance how progress will be measured.

2. Have a plan

Put it on paper. Like most business start-ups, NFPs should also write their plan out in the form of a report or a presentation. Key to this process is homework; research, research, research. It is just as important for NFPs to write a formal document as it is with a for-profit business and the content of the plan should have many similarities to a formal business plan; an executive summary, a description of the market space and size, competitive analysis, and projections of growth and description of how that growth will be measured.

3. Understand your market

Many NFPs don't view their organization as being a participant in a market, but the truth is they are. A market merely defines the aggregate of demand for a product or service and every organization, whether for profit or not participates in one. Without a clear understanding of your market, its size, shape, and composition it is impossible to define goals, raise funds, or execute strategy.

4. Market modestly

It is necessary for NFPs to put a great deal of thought into their audience or audiences and then look for simple ways to market to each segment. For instance a service oriented NFP might have two types of 'customer,' donors and clients, and the strategy, messaging, and tactics to reach each of those may be very different. For each of these groups, it is necessary to understand what it will take to 'convert' a customer by building awareness, providing education, and making interaction as simple and barrier-free as possible.

5. Get online

If your potential customers are looking for you, whether you are aware of them or not, it is critical that your organization have an online presence. Whether your website allows you to process transactions, gather contact information, provide educational content, or simply manage your own internal process, its very existence is beneficial. Creating, maintaining, mining, and leveraging the website can be done in many ways but in the new millennium the lack of a website is a competitive and practical disadvantage.

6. Leverage the crowd

Like start-ups and small business everywhere, NFPs can take advantage of crowd sourcing for everything from decretive services to fundraising, to professional services like accounting and public relations. Sites like Kickstarter allow NFPs and others to post their requests for funding and puts those requests in front of a large network of donors who can choose which organization, project, or effort they wish to help. Other organizations, like the taproot foundation, help NFPs connect with professional service providers for pro-bono help with legal, marketing, and other critical areas.

7. Mine your data

Just as businesses large and small use analytics tools to understand their traffic, their customers, and their conversion metrics, NFPs can also benefit from the tools used for this. And there are some great ones out there, many of them completely free. For instance, Google has a suite of tools available that NFPs can use as effectively as start-ups and small businesses; AdWords Small Business Centre, Google Analytics, Google Alerts, and Google Places are all tools which can be used to great effect.

8. Be a leader

Being a leader in your market or space is not only about innovating, but also about sharing your knowledge, advocating for your believes, and building your network. To do these effectively requires you to be a leader in action, but also a leader in thought. Create content, promote your public face, and make connections. Great tools are easily available to help: create a blog and post regularly, develop an email newsletter strategy, share resources, ideas, articles, and connections on Twitter, leverage Facebook to keep your audience and clients up to date on your efforts and activities, and identify conferences, classrooms, and other venues for speaking opportunities. When others look to you for your opinion, your analysis, or your ideas, be ready to provide them any way you can.

Viral Effect of Marketing and Not-for-Profit Gold

I spend a fair amount of time on social media websites. I check into Facebook several times on any given day, I follow over 700 people on my Twitter account and average anywhere from 3-10 posts to it per day. I also regularly visit LinkedIn as well as Google+ and have been known to browse Pinterest,

Quora, and some of the various other players. The point is that I usually have a pretty good feel when a topic is trending or a movement is growing on the Internet. At dinner this past Tuesday, my 15 year old son asked me if anyone at work was talking about that "Coney video." I had no idea what he was talking about and asked him what he meant; "There is this guy in Africa and he is been kidnapping kids and forcing them to fight. Don't worry you will hear about it soon" Ah, That Kony. I was aware of the Lord's Resistance Army through various news accounts over the past 5 years, but wasn't aware of a web video. My son went on to tell me that lots of kids at his high school had been talking about the video and the group that was promoting it and they were horrified by what they learned.

The video that my son and his friends had seen was the culmination of a sophisticated and strategic effort to build awareness and raise money for a very specific cause. The web has seen other videos go viral, but never with the speed accomplished by three young filmmakers who travelled to Africa in 2003 to help stop the rebel Joseph Kony's ferocious campaign and his strategy of using children as soldiers and sex slaves. It took them 8 years of work to shoot, edit and distribute the film, but in the past week, it has turned Kony into a familiar name to tens of millions of people around the world. The filmmaker's organization, Invisible Children, launched the Kony 2012 video on Monday and, as of this writing, the video had received over 100 million views on YouTube. It has been mentioned on Facebook over 400,000 times, more than 2.8 million users have Liked the page and by the end of last week the Twitter hashtag #StopKony had been used over 10 million times.

Invisible Children was formed in 2003 and has produced 11 films to date. Before launching the Stop Kony effort, they had already amassed a sizable following in the social media and it was this young, passionate base that they leveraged to launch the Kony 2012 effort. Their strategy was to get their followers to share the film through their own personal networks, and to enlist celebrities and others with large SM followings to help get the word out about the film and to share the link with anyone they could. Their simple message was "capture Kony," and their call to action was a specific request to viewers to share it through their own networks on social media platforms and to make the name "Kony" ubiquitous on the web. This idea of joining in the hunt by clicking the "share" button was simple and allowed people, especially young people, to feel that they were involved and doing something positive by simply using a tool that they use every day of their lives.

Invisible Children's goal was also straightforward: to put pressure on the Ugandan government and other African countries to capture Kony by the end of 2012. Within days, the effort was paying off mightily on Monday the VansWarpedTour twitter feed was tweeting about the video and soon other entertainment industry figures followed suit: Taylor Swift, Alec Baldwin, and Rihanna all started sharing the link and on Tuesday Oprah Winfrey tweeted it out to her 9.7 million followers and then posted multiple updates in the following days. On Tuesday it was Ryan Seacrest and Justin Bieber to his 18 million followers. Even Kim Kardashian got into the fray and brought along another 13 million Twitter users.

The effort, however, has not been without some controversy and social media pushback. Some questioned whether the effort was over-simplifying the situation and others pointed out that Kony was no longer in Uganda. Still others question whether Invisible Children is completely transparent in its fundraising and in communicating how the money they raise is being used, with debate about whether the filmmakers are calling for military intervention in a delicate diplomatic and political situation.

Overall though, the social media effort launched by Invisible Children has made a huge impact and can be studied as an object lesson in leveraging the web and an organization's followers to promote a single issue, to encourage action on the part of those followers, and to build worldwide awareness to bring justice to a small corner of the world.

Chapter 17: Some Tips On Doing the Right Thing

Earlier in this book I wrote about some ways that not-for-profits could leverage the concepts of lean marketing. In this chapter I would like to discuss ways that small business can support not-for-profits and get involved in meaningful causes, and at the same time help to drive economic development locally, regionally, or even internationally. The non-profit benefits from increased promotion to a larger audience and the small business can benefit from positive public relations, stronger audience engagement, and marketing opportunities that they might not otherwise have.

This strategy has come to be known as Cause Marketing, and it typically describes how a business engages with a not-for-profit organization to the benefit of both. A great example of this is (PRODUCT) RED campaign, a major marketing effort, the goal of which was to help eliminate AIDS in Africa. Major brands, including Nike, Gap, Starbucks, and Apple among other large companies, signed on to this effort and shared the (Product) Red logo on their products, and in their advertising and branding. Small business, too, can engage in similar efforts through local charities such as United Way, March of Dimes, and the Red Cross. These organizations allow businesses to cross-promote their efforts and use the NFPs branding to indicate their participation.

As you consider whether Cause Marketing is a good strategy for your business, the most important point to remember is that first you have to believe in the cause. Don't choose a non-profit because you think it will help you reach more customers, but rather because you believe in the work they are doing. Don't promote a social effort because you believe you can profit from that effort, but rather because it is something that is important to you. In other words, let the cause itself drive your involvement, and let the marketing impact remain secondary. Your customers will appreciate your passion, your involvement and your integrity and it is out of this admiration that they may be compelled to support your business.

Here are a few businesses that have actually built a meaningful following around a cause and that contribute greatly to communities around the world.

1. Grameen Bank makes small (micro) loans to poor people to help them start their own businesses.
2. NIKA Water Company sells bottled water in the USA and uses its profits to bring clean water to the developing world.
3. Newman's Own donates 100% of its profits to support educational charities.
4. Toms Shoes sells lightweight shoes and with every pair sold, donates a pair to a person in need.

We encourage you to finds a cause you care about and engage your employees, your family, your friends, and your customers. They will appreciate your passion and your efforts, and you will be proud of your own engagement and effort for an undertaking you believe in. And, if all goes well, your business will prosper as a result of your work. Remember, what comes around, goes around.

Chapter 18: Conclusion

Small businesses and start-ups face many challenges when marketing their products and services.

Small businesses and start-ups have minimal brand recognition, are often located in geographic or demographic areas that limit their marketing options, and most have small (or non-existent) marketing budgets.

Some marketers advise small businesses and start-ups to research and create strategic marketing plans. Such plans can help and strategy is important. But strategic marketing plans take time, resources and money. Few young companies cannot afford that cost.

Other marketers recommend that small businesses and start-ups build a website or optimize their existing website, develop email lists, start blogging, and develop newsletters. These tactics can be important and may work for some, but they also require time, resources and money.

The reality is that for the vast majority of small businesses and start-ups, marketing consists of handing out a business card.

Why?

Marketing and advertising require an investment of significant amounts of money and time. The ads we see on television or in magazines, for example, were developed by agencies and consultants who evaluated past campaigns, developed concepts and assumptions about advertising themes, conducted some market research/focus group testing, created story boards, developed scripts (for commercials), and much more. It's no surprise that the cost of running the advertising itself is often smaller than the cost to produce that ad or marketing piece.

The truth is that most advertising and marketing doesn't work. Studies show that people ignore online ads and other forms of advertising are not much better.

Yet products and services rarely sell themselves; small businesses and start-ups must find ways to let their potential customers know about those products and services.

In this post, we are going to explore several strategies small businesses and start-ups can leverage when marketing their products or services without spending a lot of money or time developing comprehensive marketing plans.

First, some background for those not familiar with lean start-up principles. "Lean Start-up" reflects a set of key principles used by some entrepreneurs to quickly and inexpensively develop new products and services. Lean start-up principles promote creating rapid prototypes of your products and services designed to test your assumptions about the market and then to rely on feedback from customers to enhance those products and services.

There's strong support for the lean start-up movement in the marketplace, including from investors. Even agencies have taken notice and are talking about ways that agencies can apply lean start-up principles when they counsel their clients.

What can small businesses and start-ups learn from lean start-up principles?

Let's take three key elements of lean start-up principles; quick and inexpensive prototypes that test market assumptions, feedback from real customers, and learn fast, don't fail fast – and apply those elements to strategies for small businesses and start-up marketing.

Test your marketing ideas in small batches

Many small business owners and entrepreneurs think that picking the right marketing channel will solve all of their problems. But there is no one right marketing channel for all businesses. Some products and services sell better using one channel, while others sell better using different marketing strategies and tactics.

By trying different tactics, you will get a better sense of where your customers are, how they respond to your marketing messages, and how they like your products and services. Once you start excluding things that don't work after a period of testing, you can focus more of your energy and budget on the marketing channels that are effective for your company.

Instead of starting with big strategic marketing plans and investing huge portions of your marketing budget on one or two initiatives, break your budget into small pieces that you can use to test various marketing ideas. For example, you could set aside some funds to experiment with offline and online promotions, online small business listing sites, referral programs, deal-of-the-day sites like Groupon, print ads in local papers or mailers, online ads, hyper-local advertising on Facebook, participation on Twitter, or adwords on Google. Decide on a small budget for each effort, set a reasonable time frame (at AA Global Sourcing, we typically experiment with most marketing initiatives for two weeks but there are exceptions), and then monitor and assess the results, although be careful to focus on the important information.

Listen to your customers

Perhaps the most important lean start-up lesson for small businesses and start-ups is the need to increase the frequency of contact with real customers. Marketing is often directed at a faceless, voiceless audience and you rarely, if ever, hear from that audience. It's the equivalent of standing on top of a tall building with a megaphone and talking loudly about your company. How likely is it that such a strategy would work?

Small businesses and start-ups don't have big budgets to blanket the world with their marketing messages. So what can they do?

We advise small businesses and start-ups to maximize social media. Build a community, support them, and leverage them. Market WITH not TO your community. This is sound advice and is in stark contrast to the way most companies market. Companies rarely engage in dialogue with their customers and as a result, miss opportunities to learn and improve their products and services.

Learn fast, don't fail fast

Many people fear failure. For most, this fear is healthy because not every failure is a learning experience. But the key to lean marketing for small businesses and start-ups is to focus on learning, not failure. The goal is to learn as much as you can about your marketing options and spend as little money and energy as possible to gain that knowledge. While many of your marketing tests may fail (at AA Global Sourcing, 99% of the marketing programs we try don't work out), you will be able to adjust, refocus, and find marketing channels that work. And importantly, by applying lean marketing principles and focusing on small, iterative initiatives and feedback from your customers, you will test your theories and assumptions within weeks or months, while your competitors will wait years to see if their grand bet-the-company marketing initiative succeeds or fails.

Good Luck!

Resource and References

Shigeo Shingo, Norman Bodek, Collin McLoughlin: Kaizen and the Art of Creative Thinking - The Scientific Thinking Mechanism

Shigeo Shingo; Fundamental Principles of Lean Manufacturing

Shigeo Shingo, Andrew P. Dillon (Translator); Zero Quality Control: Source Inspection and the Poka-yoke System

Shigeo Shingo; Non-Stock Production: The Shingo System of Continuous Improvement

Shigeo Shingo; A Study of the Toyota Production System from an Industrial Engineering Viewpoint

Shigeo Shingo; A Study of the Toyota Production System from an Industrial Engineering Viewpoint

Drucker, P. (1993) Post-Capitalist Society

Drucker, P., "What Makes an Effective Executive", Harvard Business review, June 2004

Lessons from Toyota's long drive, an interview with Katsuaki Watanabe, HBR, July 2007

Liker, J. & D. Meier, Toyota Talent, McGraw Hill, 2007

Shook, J. , Managing To Learn, Lean Enterprise Institute 2008

Fishman, C., "No Satisfaction", Fast Company, Dec 2006/Jan 2007

Womack, J. & J. Shook, Lean Management and The Role of Lean Leadership, Lean Enterprise Institute presentation, Oct. 2006

www.ingramcontent.com/pod-product-compliance
Lightning Source LLC
Chambersburg PA
CBHW051729170526
45167CB00002B/867